Understanding Business

By: Fred Schlissel ©
1/2/14

The Axioms Of Business

Axiom: A statement or proposition that is regarded as being established, accepted or self-evident

About the Author

Fred Schlissel has had an exceptional, successful, and productive career.

Starting as an industrial engineer, he soon became key **executive** in a fast moving company where he was in complete charge of all manufacturing.

He moved on to a continuing consulting career where he served as **consultant** to over 50 companies in a dozen industries. He worked directly the owner/entrepreneurs of client companies. His work with clients extended for 10, 15 and 20 years of continuous consulting engagements testifying to his recognized contribution to these clients.

He was, concurrent with the above, and Adjunct **Professor** of Management and Entrepreneurship at NYU, Columbia, Fordham, Baruch, Hofstra and more.

He is an **entrepreneur** having started AutoWoopie, Inc., an internet service company for the 200,000,000 automobile owners in the U. S.

He is the **author** of articles on management, a children's book
"Why The Wind Loves Children", a science fiction book "Bublonya" and now this book "Axioms of Business

Dedication

With the greatest of pleasure I dedicate this book to Betty Schlissel, the most caring of women, yet independent and a contributor to her profession, her family and, most of all, to me. As my wife, she is my love, friend, companion, helpmate as well as loving and caring mother and grandmother.

Acknowledgements

I thank my wife, Betty, for proof reading this book and making the many corrections that my sloppy style created.

I thank my brother, Martin Schlissel Ph.D., for his many insights and suggestions that added more depth to my thinking.

I thank my son, Arnold Schlissel, an accomplished professional video editor, for his invaluable technical help in preparing this book for publication

Axioms of Business

Understanding Business

By: Fred Schlissel ©
1/2/14

"In the midst of events there is no perspective"
Barbra Tuchman

The Axioms Of Business

Axiom: A statement or proposition that is regarded as being established, accepted or self-evident

Axiom #1

The "Business" of America is Business *

Oscar Wilde, in one of his plays wrote of: "**A man who knows the price of everything and the value of nothing**". I respectfully disagree…up to a point. I believe that the vast majority of people have no inkling of the price of anything, and value nothing. They prefer to think and act as though everything in the world is free. They do not understand that there is an economic basis for everything that is done. To put it most simply: there is a cost to everything we do. These economic factors, these costs may even be hidden, subtle, even unknown. Yet, and without exception, the economics of every situation is a force that eventually must be reckoned with. Someone, someplace, some time is paying a bill for something for someone who was unaware that there was a price to be paid.

This economic force manifests itself with three factors:

1) Work – everything we do requires work that must be done by us or by others, directly or indirectly.
2) Money – there is a cost, or price for everything that is done. Money flows and we must allow for it.
3) Value - this means that what we do considering 1) & 2) above must make sense. In this case that means we must have a sense of the value of our activity. The work and the money involved have to be worth it. An imbalance between work and money means inefficiency, waste of resources and probable failure.

A trip to the library is free, but someone is paying for it.

A visit to a park is free, but someone is paying for it.

School is free, but someone is paying for it.

The air we breathe is free, but someone is paying to keep it pure.

Water is free, but someone is paying for it.

We listen to the radio. It's free, but someone pays for it.

We don't think about the cost of so many things. We just take for granted that they are free.

In addition, we have no sense of the value of the most common things we do. We take for granted that they are just there for us to use or consume without regard for their cost, or the effort necessary to provide them.

This is human nature that we cannot change, but we must also understand it. You see, we may be the ones paying the bill. Someone must know and act and fund the cost and value of what I call the "business" of living.

I have been in many situations where valuable, trusted, experienced employees perform their work with no concept that there is cost and effort involved with their activity. They are exceptionally competent at their work, yet are oblivious to the "business" aspects of their work. They get paid for working, but are otherwise not conscious of the cost of their activity. What does waste mean if there is no understanding of cost? What does efficiency or productivity mean in the absence of a sense of value? This widespread failure to understand and acknowledge the cost or value of a business activity can be a deterrent in attempts to control cost, increase productivity and efficiency.

It is quite appropriate for the business owner to make cost, or cost relationships a known factor in an employees' work. With a little creativity it is possible to construct systems for employees at work so that not only are they made aware of the costs of their activity, but they are also given a sense of "ownership" of those costs. If an employee can be made to understand and acknowledge cost in their work, and accept responsibility for those costs, it behooves the employee to control those costs. A cleverly designed system will give employees a financial stake in cost control, so that the employee has an incentive to maintain or reduce operational costs.

For society, it makes taxation much more difficult if taxpayers have little or no appreciation for the cost and value of the services paid for by their taxes. Taxation is even more complicated because taxpayers are often paying for services they do not use directly, but are used by other members of society, just not them. It is difficult for people, even well intentioned people, to raise above the "what's in it for me?" syndrome. The cost of living, the "business" of living in a modern society is complicated and difficult for average taxpayers to understand, yet the costs have to be paid by someone. It should be the responsibility of government – politicians - to explain how tax payments are put to use to benefit all members of society, and how all taxpayers are made stronger when all of "us" are made whole, or prosper. The problem is that most politicians are not clever enough to make these explanations, or are corrupt and do not wish to expose themselves.

*Attributed to Calvin Coolidge

Axiom #2

Business is Like a Contact Sport.

People get hurt. There are winners and losers. The better prepared and better trained are more likely to win. The unexpected always happens: an injury, bad weather, an error or penalty or mistake in the field. A good recovery from something unexpected is the sign of a winner.

This describes sports, but it is also a metaphor for business that is also bruising and fast moving.

Competitors constantly try to keep you off balance. They do the unexpected, the unusual. They play in your field, with your customers. They don't ask for permission. They use their elbows and their whole bodies to beat you, to take advantage, to be first. And, of course, you do the same to them. Any thing can happen at any time to give you a kick where it can hurt. A key employee suddenly becomes a competitor. A supplier breaks down. Someone steals. You are found to violate safe business practices. A severe storm suddenly knocks out your communications, or electricity. A new material obsoletes your product. Machine parts are delayed. You have banking or financial problems. Customers become fickle. Trends change. You are caught lagging by a disruptive technology.

I cannot begin to list all of the things that put a business at great risk, that are like body blows, causing massive economic damage. They are ever present, ever threatening. There is almost no protection from business risk. You can only hope that you have enough reserves of money, of time, of intellect, of human stamina for a make over, to recover, to regain lost momentum and restore your business position.

Thus, the successful, forward thinking entrepreneur builds financial reserves for some inevitable, unexpected – and unwelcome – challenge. He/she is prepared for injury and anticipates eventual recovery.

The Capitalistic system isn't for sissies. It is fast moving, volatile, unpredictable, changeable, battered by competition, fragile and on and on with risks upon risks. Yet this is the strength of the system, as well: flexibility, adaptability, rapid responsiveness, constantly self-renewing, and self-correcting. The economist Joseph Schumpeter popularized the theme of creative destruction meaning that the capitalistic economic system is in constant motion destroying what exists as it simultaneously creates something new, and hopefully better.

It's a very harsh system with pain for those who cannot keep up, or who are too slow to adapt. There are winners and losers, and, interestingly, switches between them. A winner today can easily become a loser tomorrow, and sometimes it flips the other way. The successful entrepreneur is on his/her game all the time. There is no time off. Those who become weary, or lose their mettle lose the "game" and it's over for them, but there is a new game in town for the next group of highly motivated, energetic, creative risk taking entrepreneurs. The process repeats. The "game" goes on.

Note that this very system of success and failure, winning, loosing and renewal allowed the capitalistic system to survive and flourish. Capitalism created the greatest prosperity and improved the living standards for all. However, it is true results are uneven and not everyone benefited from the system, but we're not finished yet! Conversely, the competing economic systems of socialism and communism were tried, proved sclerotic and unresponsive and eventually failed, but not before the leaders did great harm to their people and set society back for generations. Think of the lost opportunity. Both China and the former Soviet Union have abandoned their Communist economic system, embraced Capitalism, and their societies have made great strides forward.

]

Axiom #3

The sole purpose of a business is to <u>satisfy</u> the <u>needs and wants</u> of a <u>customer</u>.

It seems so elementary, but it is so overlooked. The whole purpose of being in business is to provide some goods or service that some one needs or wants, that they are willing to buy and pay for. It isn't about you at all. You may think that all of the effort, all of the risk puts your interests at the front of the line. Of course you think that. You're the one who makes every thing happen. You've worked so hard. Sacrificed so much.

Dangerous thinking

.

It is all about having a customer who is willing to pay a market price for your offerings. *It's always about the customer*. It is not necessary to make a customer happy, because happiness is a temporary state of mind and very changeable. Your objective should be to <u>satisfy</u> your customers. Satisfaction lingers. It has a memory. The customer is satisfied with some combination of price, quality and service. Competitive success in business requires superiority in at least one of these attributes. The clever businessperson soon understands which attribute can be most successful considering the market place and the balance of the resources the company has available. Then through hard work, careful planning and adroit execution it may be possible to achieve marketing superiority.

A successful business will know who their customers are, and how to satisfy them. Yet most businesses do not know who their customers are. Of course, they know them by name probably, but can they identify their customers by category or industry segment or other classification, which is powerful marketing information.

Most companies do not know why customers do business with them. What competitive advantage does your company have from the perspective of your customer? What is it about your company that they like? The Scottish poet Robert Burns put it best. *"Oh, what a great gift we would have if we could only see ourselves as others see us"*. The reverse is also valuable but more difficult to know, that is, why potential customers do <u>not</u> do business with you. Harold Arlen and Johnny Mercer wrote a popular song with these lyrics *"you got to accentuate the positive and eliminate the negative"*. This is great insight from a poet and great advice from songsters.

Customers have needs, things that they really have a current need for, and other things that they want – those things that will make their lives more complete, or beautiful, or somehow fulfilled. It is only by satisfying a need or want that induces a customer to make a purchase. Yet needs and wants are volatile, changeable, even emotional and often unpredictable. To make it more complicated, as if that was necessary, all customers within the same marketplace are likely to have different needs or wants at the same time.

Needs and wants change over time, by technological advances and by whim. In an essay about management and leadership the iconic management expert, Peter Drucker, quotes one of his teacher's, speaking about World War 1, who said, *"Not enough General were killed"*, meaning that the generals stayed behind the lines and did not know what was going on at the front lines and therefore lost their battles. Yet this is exactly how a company knows about customer needs and wants and their changeability. The true entrepreneur engages with his/her customers and reaches out to them and constantly gages their needs and wants, and the changing dynamics of the marketplace. This is a continuing task without letup. In the Broadway musical "The Music Man" the chorus sings a song about how traveling salesmen must *"know the territory"*.

And so it is with customers. A company must have intimate and continuing knowledge of their customers, who their customers are, why they buy, what satisfies them and has continuing contemporary insight into the customers changing needs and wants, because the sole purpose of a business is to <u>satisfy</u> the <u>needs and wants</u> of a <u>customer</u>.

Axiom #4

Profit is a reward for excellence.

This is the only way to think about profits. Yes, some times profit is a result of opportunism, being in the right place at the right time. Or, profit may result from a successful speculation. But for the successful company that has a long-term perspective and understands the importance of continuity, profit is a reward for being very great - excellent – at what you do. It is exceptional performance that results in long term continuing profitability. This means operational performance. Every part of the company performs at some optimum peak. Simply put, this refers to administration, management, operations, sales and marketing.

Performance is not an abstract term. It means that <u>people</u> are performing at this highest level and achieving exceptional results.

What a challenge!

Selecting the right people and inspiring and motivating them; having the right high attainable goals for them to strive for; measuring their progress. It means having in place a system of incentives and rewards.

Is it possible to run a company this way on a continuing basis?

It starts with a realization that company profits are a reward – result – of being very well run. That means long-term excellent performance. It requires staffing the company with talented people who are capable of achieving superior high level of performance. It continues with having and articulating suitable goals, and methods in place designed for the results intended. It requires recognition of exceptional performance with a fair system of compensation including incentives and performance-based rewards.

Long-term continuing profits come from hard work driven by a superior strategy.

There are many ways of thinking about profits. Most commonly they are a measure of the operating success of the company. It allows comparison of a company's success with that of peer companies. The profit trend over time provides a sense of continuity and indicates stability and managerial competence. Profits also measure the return on invested capital. This allows owners to compare their investment in the company with alternatives investment opportunities. Profits are needed to offset the risks that are inherent with any business venture. The higher risk should be compensated with higher profits. Profits are the reward to the entrepreneur for innovation, personal effort, and risk for the venture. It provides the entrepreneur with the opportunity for well-deserved wealth accumulation. Profits are essential in providing long term financing for the company, as well as short-term day-to-day operating capital. In capitalism there is no substitute for profits. The economic system is nurtured by profits.

Competent people and a culture of operating excellence promote profitable performance. However, having managerial controls in place that quickly identify operating aberrations are necessary for quick response so that rapid corrections can be made. This is almost a formula for excellent performance: good, highly motivated people in place with quick response controls that allow the people to make timely corrections. Strangely, however, it may contain elements of its own destruction. The operating system that is so successful, under certain circumstances, can be the cause of its very downfall. There is an inherent contradiction to be aware of. Efficiency requires repetition and attention to the smallest details and constant incremental improvement. So far so good. The danger lies in tunnel vision. This intense concentration on operating details can rob good people of their broad-spectrum creative powers. Their "ownership" of the efficient operating processes that they designed, that they take pride in, prevents them from seeing the "big picture", which may reveal a whole new and better way to get the job done. They are so captivated by their success, that they fail to reinvent, renew, review, rebuild, restore, remodel, replace. So operating excellence can inadvertently contain the seeds of its own destruction. This potential failure can be avoided. The truly excellent company builds change, renewal and creative thinking right into its operating system. People can be switched around so that a new perspective is introduced. Outside experts can be asked to make evaluations. A culture of intellectual innovation can be made part of the normal thinking of the people who run the company, and through them, passed on to every one in the company. And, in this way, profits are really earned for excellence in operations and continuing excellence.

Axiom #5

The most important job of the owner/entrepreneur is to grow the business and adapt to change.

There is nothing in life that is permanent or stagnant. Everything is in constant motion, rising, falling, twisting, changing. It is only the limitations of the human mind, the mind that seeks calm over chaos, stability over transformation that prevents so many people from understanding that high velocity change is the way of life…the grand design, if there is such a thing.

Nowhere is this system of continuous change more evident than in the field of business where financial success – or failure - is so easily and often measured by a dollar sign.

Recognizing that long-term business stagnation leads only to failure what is an entrepreneur to do? There is no choice: either grow the business or fail.

Choose growth. It's more satisfying.

The entrepreneurial process is mysterious in the sense that no one can fully understand what inner forces, or demons, drive the entrepreneur. We know this much: t-he entrepreneur recognizes – senses, or has some vision about a market need, a customer need or want, that is unfulfilled, and conceives of a unique way of filling that need. The entrepreneur has the drive, imagination, persistence, and so many other skills, including a tolerance for risk that can result in a new business formation.

Failure is always looking over the shoulder of the entrepreneur. The vast majority of new businesses fail within five years. These statistics do not deter the true entrepreneur. An entrepreneur never fails. The business may fail for a variety of reasons. But the entrepreneur, the person with all of the talent, never fails. Undertaking an entrepreneurial venture with all of the accompanying doubts and risks is, in itself, a success – a huge success!

So we know that the entrepreneur who successfully starts a new business has the right ability.

We also know that the existing business is constantly beset by mostly unknowable forces: competition, changing customers with changing needs, new technology, legal and environmental issues, human limitations, etc. etc. etc.

The company cannot stagnate because the conditions in which it operates wont allow it.

An entrepreneur can be resistant to change, but this is ultimately futile.

There is no choice. Adapt to change and grow the business or risk failure.

The entrepreneur must be the leader in adapting to change.

Sometimes the entrepreneur succumbs to human failure. The entrepreneur can become tired and lose drive, or vision. He/she can become complacent and lose opportunity seized by others. He/she can become arrogant with success and looses vision. He/she can become frightened and thus loose everything. There is a natural life cycle to every business. First, a new company may experience rapid growth in the early phase of the company's business cycle. The second phase is maturity: success and continuity. Surprisingly, this is the most dangerous phase of the company's business cycle. It can lead to complacency, a sense of "having made it", mistaking success, which is temporary, for inevitability, and, misguidedly they rest on nonexistent laurels. Three things can happen to a company at this phase in the business cycle. First, it can enter long-term stagnation and coast along on momentum for some time. Second, it can go into decline quickly. Third, the mark of the real successful company is to start the entrepreneurial process over again. The original entrepreneur may get a second wind and go on to bigger and even better things. The original founding entrepreneur may have trained or brought on board other people with entrepreneurial drive. A highly selective and careful acquisition of another rapidly growing company in it's early stage of it's business cycle may help to restore entrepreneurial energies to the original company. And thus, the entrepreneurial cycle renews and the company starts a new cycle and has a new lease on life.

Regardless of technique, the successful entrepreneur understands that entrepreneurship is a continuing process that must be a constant force devoted to growing the business.

He does this through relentless innovation of process and product, and recognizing and seizing new opportunities.

A time may come, through fault or no fault, when economic or business conditions collapse. It is vitally important that the business owner recognizes these conditions very early. Delay may result in an inability to employ defensive strategy. The entrepreneur must know, or sense when these threats are present - the entrepreneur's prime responsibility becomes protecting the assets of the company. Whatever it means. Whatever it takes. Survival. This requires a thoughtful strategy whereby asset s and liabilities are weighed and assessed, considering long-term issues regarding the future viability of the company. The very structure of the company, its products or services and markets need to be considered objectively, intellectually without favoritism or emotions. If these dire conditions manifest themselves there is only one goal: survival, whatever it takes.

When is the best time to do survival planning? When it's not necessary. When everything is good. When the extreme pressures of the moment do not hang over the company owner-operators like an imminent threat, like pending disaster. Clear eyed, dispassionate reasoning, when there is no threat present, is the best time for survival planning, but *have a plan.*

Axiom #6

Innovation is the driving force of business success and growth.

Diversity is a natural force of all life. I don't know how many different species there are on our planet, but lots: birds, fish, animals, plants, insects, and certainly people. And think of how many, many varieties there are within each species. It's really a fun exercise.

On one level, we are accustomed to things being different. We expect choices. We want to select the things we want or need. We like variety. Look at a crowd of people. Do you ever see anyone wearing the same clothing as someone else in the crowd? Never! Variety. And through the process of creating variety we also make things better. We improve as we go along. This process is called innovation, making or designing things with ingenuity, originality, and inventiveness – something new and different from what exists. This is a process that allows the entrepreneur to distinguish his product or service from competitors thus creating a competitive edge. Innovation is not the same as invention. Invention is a new discovery. Innovation usually means putting existing things together in new ways, with changes, perhaps introducing some breakthrough not previously thought of.

On another level, we resist change. As natural as diversity is in all of life, the creative process of innovation is natural, as well. Yet it takes a fight – a vicious fight – to innovate and to be an innovator. The entrepreneur must fight the cobwebs of conformity, must think about things in new ways, must be willing experiment starting with his own mind. The fight continues. The surest way to invite condemnation and ridicule is to talk about a new innovative idea. How you will be vilified! Laughed at – perhaps condemned. That's why the entrepreneur must be a visionary. A visionary sees things that others do not see. The visionary has the power and conviction to first drive through his own forces of resistance, and then go forward fighting the resistance – the lack of understanding or foresight of everyone else. A daunting task indeed.

But there is no choice because innovation is the driving force behind business growth and success. Plus, of course, there is the euphoria that comes with discovery of the new.

There is nothing like it!

The successful person in business is more than an innovator. He encourages all around him to become innovative thinkers. Think of the power and potential for good if many people in an enterprise are thinking of new ways, better ways, improved ways of getting things done. This is the task of the most successful entrepreneurs and managers.

Everyone in the business must be challenged to create new ideas for every part of the business, and then be motivated to work hard to implement them.

Innovation is not mysterious. It may appear so, but it's not. Breakthrough ideas can come from anyone – everyone! No one has a monopoly on innovation. We all have the ability and the capacity to be clever innovators.

I'll prove it to you.

Look at children at play. Give them a piece of paper, a string, a crayon - give them anything, the most unlikely of things. Then look at what they do with them. They invent. They fantasize. They make believe. They create. They have fun by letting their minds take off in any direction. Children are natural born innovators. Why? Because they haven't been told what they can or cannot do. There are no constraints on their minds or their thinking. They do not yet know what the "right" things are. They are free to think whatever their minds can imagine.

We were all children once. Born with the innate ability to innovate, to discover, to think freely. What a blessing! As we grow up we learn about all of the processes and procedures of adulthood. We absorb the norms of society: what's- good and bad, what's expected of us, what can and cannot be done.

The effect is to depress our natural born ability to innovate and create. We go with the flow!

It's so much simpler to be like everyone else in what we do, wear, think, say, etc. But in so doing we stifle one of our greatest human gifts: innovative thinking.

But be of good cheer. Our ability to innovate is merely suppressed. It is not destroyed. It is up to us to reclaim this natural ability. We can engage in specific exercises like brainstorming. We can just force ourselves to think "out-of-the-box". We can write down lists of ideas, lots of them. Sort them out later. In an article published in The Harvard Business Review in the spring of 1985, Peter Drucker writes "In innovation as in any other endeavor, there is talent, there is ingenuity, and there is knowledge. But when all is said and done, what innovation requires is hard, focused, purposeful work.". The title of Drucker's article is "The Discipline of Innovation". We can train ourselves, force ourselves to become innovators. Let the child within each of us reemerge and oh! What fun we can have! How productive we can be! What we will be able to create to benefit society and ourselves! One never knows.

Edison, America's original mechanical genius, is reputed to have said, " Genius is one per cent inspiration and ninety-nine percent perspiration. Thomas Jefferson, and some others, supposedly said, "The harder I work the luckier I am."

There is plenty of evidence telling us that innovation and creative thinking are widely possible. One needs the recognition that innovation is a societal good, the drive to force the mind into a creative mode, the hard work and persistence to achieve an original thought break through, the ability to accept inevitable frustration and even failure, all to enjoy the eventual eureka experience of success! There's no tonic, no elixir like having a great idea.

You can do it.

Axiom #7

Nothing is forever

Surely we are not forever. What we invent or create is not forever and may be coopted at any time. Our energies and tolerance for risk may not be forever, or even last very long. We can fortunately leave a legacy. Our progeny is one type of legacy. A successful on going business is another form of legacy. What we want to avoid is a declining business, or worse, a failed business for others to cannibalize.

Thus, you have to know when to get out.

A college professor asked his students, "When do you leave the Party?" Of course, they all answered when the party was over. "No", he said, "If you wait until it's over, all you remember is that you were tired, ate or drank too much, and couldn't wait to get home."

"You leave the party at its peak. Then you remember what a great party it was, and what a great time you were having."

"You leave the party when you're having the most fun."

So it is with an enterprise. You have to know when to pass it along to others with new energy, new ideas and a new outlook. I know how easy it is to make this recommendation, and how hard it is to carry out. After all, it is your creation, the result of your hard work, your creativity, the risks you overcame. Who can possibly be good enough, talented enough to carry on without you? It's so hard to avoid being personally and emotionally caught up in – consumed – by your enterprise. Yet nothing is forever. What it amounts to is not when or if you will pass it along - because by force of nature you will – but rather the circumstances by which you will pass it along. Will you leave a legacy? What kind of legacy will it be? If you are proactive you can control the process for your maximum benefit. If you are reactive, you take what you can. Be proactive.

Everything comes to an end. The "Ups" eventually come down. The "Downs" sometimes recover - or not. Timing is all-important. One must sense when the time is ripe to move on, to abandon what is, and avoid the painful change and inevitable decline.

Transition while your assets are fully valued. Maximize your financial return.

Leave before the party ends.

Does anyone remember Woolworth?

Axiom #8

Success cannot be guaranteed but failure can be guaranteed

There is a certain instability and unpredictability in all-human endeavor. Earthquakes, flash floods, car accidents, falls, health issues – bad things happen unexpectedly without warning. We cannot guarantee a happy or successful future. We hope for the best managing with prudence, care and resilience. And life goes on mostly with joy and happiness avoiding as best we can, life's vicissitudes. We cope with whatever resources available, fighting for a good future.

Business is even more unstable, unpredictable and uncertain. Still, business people are not deterred by risk or obstacles and roadblocks. They have visions of what might be, of potential, of building, of profits. With drive and courage they create a new enterprise mastering their fears. Yet, risk abounds from competition, disruptive technologies, market forces, financial changes, environmental causes plus human weaknesses: physical, mental, and emotional. There is the risk of incomplete information, the unknown, uncertainty and unpredictability. Hard work, thoughtful effort, careful planning, and brilliant execution---nothing can stop the unexpected from happening. Yet, in spite of obstacles, when the positive conditions do come together, success is possible, frequent and sustaining. A progressive society is built by success no matter its fragility.

We must persist.

But because of risk and uncertainty success cannot be guaranteed.

However, failure can be guaranteed.

It's easy.

Weakness, sloth, arrogance, greed, shortcuts, stupidity, bad judgment, carelessness, lack of integrity, moral turpitude, hate, impatience, lying, stealing---any one of these faults, or combination of them, guarantee failure. And who among us is so pure and innocent that we have never succumbed to these vices? To be human is also to be subject to weakness and temptation. Thus, an inability to rise above human frailty guarantees failure.

But failure can be avoided.

Failure can be avoided by understanding personal shortcomings. We have to know our own strengths and weaknesses. Failure is avoided when you avoid putting yourself into a situation that requires strengths you don't have, or amplifies the weakness you do have. I understand that you may not have the judgment that allows you to assess your situation and your ability to cope. Risk is real. You may not be successful, but try.

Success is better than failure.

Just avoiding failure is sometimes the best we can do, and may suffice.

The Entrepreneurial Manager©

By: Fred Schlissel

We need a Rosetta Stone for business owners and managers.

The Rosetta Stone was discovered in Egypt by a soldier in Napoleon's army. It contained a text translated into three languages that allowed scholars to finally read hieroglyphics.

The Rosetta Stone for business owners and managers is only a start to understanding and resolving a very critical and poorly recognized serious problem. Business owners and managers are in a symbiotic relationship. They need to work together for the successful operation of a business, an economic enterprise. And they need each other. In many ways they are like two sides of a coin. Bound to each other in a mutual dependency. Yet they have different perspectives of the company, the economic enterprise that makes it difficult for them - both the owner and the manager – to understand each other.

I've learned about this problem from my long years as a consultant to many businesses.

I recall walking through office of a large highly successful young and growing company. I was with the owner/entrepreneur as we passed the offices of his management team: the controller, chief engineer, human resources manager, production manager, sales manager, and others. All were very highly paid because the business owners' policy was to over pay his people to insure their loyalty and the extra effort that the growing business required. It was a very successful policy. As we passed their offices he said to me, almost with derision, "They're only administrators". It was a telling comment. What he meant was that all these highly paid and skilled managers – indispensible to the smooth operation of his company – were not entrepreneurs as he was and that they did not see the company from the same perspective. The language difference was not as critical as the fact that their point of reference was completely different.

The managers were interested in making sure that the company maximized profits. They had good controls in place to quickly locate discrepancies that might lead to problems. They wanted to maximize efficiency. How do you maximize efficiency? Through repetition. You do the same thing over and over again until you get it right. They wanted consistency, things to follow logically in order. They wanted predictability. They wanted to know not only what was happening, but what to expect, as well. They didn't like surprises, things that upset the stability of their little universe. They wanted open and clear communications with the owner/entrepreneur. They all worked very hard and successfully to make sure that the company was run in the best possible way.

Very commendable, even the owner/entrepreneur agreed. They were doing a good job.

But the owner/entrepreneur saw things differently. He had a different set of objectives and priorities. It's not that he didn't want the same things that his managers wanted. He did, but he wanted more. He wanted to grow the company; to continue the entrepreneurial energy, the momentum that drove the growth of the company. His managers did not understand his priorities or interests. He was eager and willing to sacrifice some of the principals of good management: consistency, cost controls, system integrity, predictability, certainty, - if it would help him to achieve his objectives. He was willing to "pay" to get his way.

His main interest was to grow the company. He understood that there were markets still to be had, expansion very possible. You expand the company by hiring more sales people, by spending for promotion, by investing in more products, which, in turn, meant investing in more capacity: expensive machines, more facilities to house the machines, inventory, research and development. This was a series of investments for the company's future. It was money put at risk in the expectation that it would help build the company and create more profits in the future. New machines and new products required new systems that were costly to install. Continuity and repetition were interrupted to make way to learn what was new. Research and development were pure costs with uncertain results. Experimentation was necessary, but costly.

The owner/entrepreneurs' attitude was to make selective risky investments in the hope of securing future profits even if it meant compromising current profits. As an entrepreneur he was a calculating risk taker.

Managers want current profits, predictability and minimum risk. As a long term, respected consultant to the company I had to spend a lot of time working individually with members of the management team on special projects, on planning, discussing problems and helping devise solutions. We became close and they often confided in me. A constant refrain was, "What is he up to now? Why is he making such dramatic changes? Why spend all that money?" I was their Rosetta Stone. Since I had intimate knowledge of the owner's plans and the reasoning behind them I "translated" the owner's plans, I rationalized the plans so that they made a certain amount of sense to the managers. They didn't have to agree, but it was important for them to understand the plans, so that they could support them. It was also good for their morale. They didn't really work for some one not in control, but whose long-range judgment was being tested, rationally.

Owner/entrepreneurs and managers have different perspectives, different priorities, and different visions. It's no wonder that they ofttimes have trouble understanding each other. The need is for more than just a Rosetta Stone to translate language differences, the need for a new understanding on both sides, a coming together of attitudes and interests.

We have to create, to train a manager who understands entrepreneurship:

The Entrepreneurial Manager

The entrepreneurial manager is a hybrid. A person highly trained and accomplished in a management skill, but who also has training and, hopefully, some experience in an entrepreneurial enterprise. This is not a far-fetched idea. There are many competent people who have all of the attributes of the entrepreneur, but who are too risk adverse to take the plunge, or who are constrained for other reasons. There are several ways to create the hybrid, the manager who is skilled enough and trained to be not only a needed professional manger, but also the willing helpmate to the entrepreneur as he tries to build the business. Not only will the entrepreneurial manager assist the entrepreneur in growing the business, but also to be the voice of reason, the warning system, checks and balances, that can prevent the entrepreneur from excess unwarranted zeal in pursuit of growth. Entrepreneurs can easily lose their perspective, and sense of proportionality as they pursue the next "big thing".

There are many university courses in entrepreneurship that examine the entrepreneurial process. They would be very helpful in the basic training of the already trained manager who wants to better understand how his boss – the owner/entrepreneur – thinks about business, and explain the entrepreneur's priorities. University courses have matured and become very vigorous in recent years and are a good starting place for any one who wants to study the subject for practical or academic reasons.

It is in the entrepreneur's interest to encourage and train managers in entrepreneurship. Not only will they understand the entrepreneur's objectives and methods, they may even contribute independent entrepreneurial ideas of their own. By so doing, the entrepreneur multiples the entrepreneurial efforts, that can be a big plus for the company. The company can only benefit by having many entrepreneurs rather than just one entrepreneur. Risks? Yes, but they can be managed.

A more direct and dynamic method for training managers to understand and contribute to the company's entrepreneurial interests is to actually create a business for the manager to operate as his/her stand-alone profit making entity. I have done this successfully many times. In one situation, we took a machine – a million dollar investment – and spun it out of its proper department and made it into a unique profit making business with a manager – now an entrepreneur in training - in charge. Machine productivity was converted into dollars representing sales, creating an income stream for the new "company". Using industrial engineering standards for productivity, material consumption, staffing and operating time we had a cost structure at standard. Beating the standards created a "profit". Sub standard productivity resulted in a "loss". The manager was now responsible for many of the tasks of the entrepreneur. He could even increase sales by scrounging more units of production for his machine from other machines in the same department. The manager and his team were given a share of the "company" "profits" as a working dividend.

This was a very successful experiment. Productivity improved, waste went down, machine time went up and staffing was reduced. Perhaps more important we trained a manager to think like an entrepreneur. This particular manager went on to become the head of one of the company's divisions.

In another instance, two actually, the companies spun off their shipping departments, which operated its own fleet of trucks, into separate stand alone for profit companies. The mangers were charged with running the "company" for a profit and were encouraged to solicit more business from other companies. In both companies, the spun off departments grew into very profitable businesses. The managers were treated like business owners and rewarded accordingly.

Another company that used a large amount of specialty chemicals a separate company was created out of the unit with its own operating entrepreneur. This spun off company was so successful that it was able to solicit extra business from the parent company's competitors.

With imagination and ingenuity, it is almost easy to create entrepreneurial opportunities for managers so that they can directly experience many important tasks that engage entrepreneurs in the real world. In the few examples above, the manager entrepreneurs were partially shielded from financial risk. Financing came from the parent company, but only if it was justified. The manager did not have his/her own money at risk, but I think that's OK. The important thing is to create a manager who can think like an entrepreneur and who understands an entrepreneurs methods and objective.

A manager who can metamorphosis into the entrepreneurial manager is no longer at odds with his boss, the owner/entrepreneur. They speak the same language. Perhaps now we do not need the Rosetta Stone after all.

In The Midst of Events There Is No Perspective ✳

By: Fred Schlissel

Here's a challenge for your imagination.

Think of yourself in the eye of a hurricane.

What would it be like for you?

In the eye of the hurricane it is calm. The sun may be shining.
The area immediately adjacent to the eye is called the eyewall with fierce winds and torrential rains causing massive destruction.
What would you be thinking while in the eye of the hurricane? Would your mind be calm like the immediate surroundings? Would your mind be in turmoil like the adjacent area?

It's interesting to contemplate, academically, but nothing I would want to actually experience.

Some years ago, I was reading a book by Barbara Tuchman, a noted historian, called "A Distant Mirror". The book was about Europe in the 14th century. It was a magnificent book and read more like a novel than one would expect of a history book. In that book Tuchman used the phrase, "In the midst of events there is no perspective". I was immediately struck by the power and truth of this very simple statement.

Everyone becomes involved with events that can cause stress. For the most part, we deal with the situation, reasonably, to a resolution, and go on with our lives. Sometimes, under certain conditions, the simple solution doesn't work out for us. It could be a sudden financial expense, or an unexpected health problem, or a family crisis, all unexpected and for which we are unprepared.

Stress, anxiety and pressure mount and demand answers, direction, solution. How do you handle it? Usually with great difficulty. The problem itself may be intractable, and beyond normal decision-making. But mostly we are stuck, as Barbra Tuchman proposes, with an inability to develop a perspective because we are entrapped by the events themselves. Raw emotions rob us of the ability to exercise any control over our circumstances. We become paralyzed by fright, uncertainty, prospect of loss and are unable to think through to a solution, although we have the capacity to do so. The stresses of the immediate events destroy our ability to react. . We make ourselves into potential victims and subject to possible abuse by some unscrupulous schemers, if we are unable to master our feelings and develop perspective.

Those in the business world are certainly and commonly subject to conditions that are tense and stressful. The economics of business thrive on change, disruption, even destruction. A business person's perspective is constantly being challenged by the rough and tumble of every day events involving customers, orders, personnel, suppliers, machines and equipment, and a myriad of day – to - day developments. Mostly they cope, perhaps complaining as they go along. They straddle the thin line between success and failure carefully, and with as much caution as they can muster.

But the businessperson cannot insulate him/her self from the occasional crunch of business, the unexpected event that blows away all sense of order. It is at this time, when clear thinking and absolute perspective is most necessary that it takes flight leaving the businessperson to flounder and become confused. Decision-making is at risk. Errors are so easy to make. Time becomes another enemy. The situation calls for action, but the business executive is confused, bewildered, at a loss about what to do. Yet everything, all the business assets, may depend upon what needs to be decided **now.**

What's to be done?

First, it's important to recognize when the situation becomes so critical that a person's judgment, perspective, becomes impaired. You have to know, instinctively, from the gut, that your ability to cope logically and sensibly is possibly compromised. You have to know when you're in trouble.

Second, time is of the essence, but use it in your favor. Try to wait it out. Perhaps the situation can be put on hold, or delayed somehow so that there is some time for events to naturally sort themselves out, or for a clearer direction to emerge from all the confusion. Play for time, if at all possible, so that your natural critical perspective is restored.

Third, change the conditions and perhaps you can change the situation so that it becomes more favorable and the crunch is avoided and your normal perspective takes over.

Fourth, get help. Don't become that bump on a log frozen into inaction and subject to external threats. It is not a show of weakness to involve others. On the contrary, it is a show of strength. Medical doctors do not treat themselves because they know that they cannot be objective – will not have clear perspective – if they are their own patients. They get help. So, too, must the businessperson under intense pressure. Talk it out with people you respect. You'd sometimes be surprised that a person from the outside, with no direct stake in the situation may have clarity of vision that eludes the person on the line. Talk to several people if necessary, until a path forward becomes apparent. It may not be what you like, but it may be what's necessary. That may be good enough under the prevailing conditions.

Most important is to understand the simple phrase by Barbara Tuchman, "In the midst of events there is no perspective".

* From Barbra Tuchman's book "A Distant Mirror"

A Statistical Conundrum©

A factoid

50% of any population that can be quantified is below average

By: Fred Schlissel

Startling, isn't it?

Yet statistics tell the whole story.

If it's height or weight it is easy to understand that there must be an average in a large body or population of people or animals, or eggs, etc. Of course, the average also means that there some are above average and some must be below average. It just so happens that half the population is below average and half is above average. This assumes a largely homogenous population. It makes sense even if you do not know statistics, and it's not hard to accept. There may be some extremes in the group, a few who may be exceptionally tall or short, or too heavy or thin, but statisticians know how to handle these exceptional situations. We don't have to bother with them.

What about intelligence? That's another matter. We can all be affected by the intelligence of the few or the many. Yes, there is some controversy about how to measure intelligence, but the statistically facts are uncontroversial. Regardless of how we may measure intelligence, there will be an average, and half the population will be above average and half will be below average.

Is this inequality or is it a natural human developmental process?

Now it gets serious.

Society – our world – has become fascinatingly complicated, technologically challenging, interconnected – in a word: complex. How does society manage – cope – when half of the people who make up society are below average? Each half has the same rights and obligations as the other half. How can society progress when half its members cannot keep up with the other half? How does a company market its products to such a widely segmented population? How does a company select effective employees from among such a medley of prospects?

Can each group contribute to society the same as the other group? The scientists, engineers, teachers, lawyers, doctors –the people upon whom society depends for progress, order, understanding, leading - even coping, do not come from those in the below average half of society as measured by intellect.

Now it gets complicated.

How does society maintain a functioning balance with such a wide dispersion of capabilities? How does society minimize conflict between those who have a greater ability to understand the issues faced by society as a whole and can contribute to resolving inherent problems, and those who have a lesser ability to understand and contribute but in other ways?

Examining statistical theory in a little more depth for insight and information two things are apparent. First, there is a cluster of data around the average. Actually, two thirds of any group – it's called a population in statistics – appear right around the center – the average. That means that the vast bulk of people in the group are average, a little below average, or a little above average. A smaller group goes beyond the average cluster in each category, above and below. Another, even smaller group, extends to the outer limits of the measurements. Thus there is an array of data clustering around the center and spreading out in both direction – above average and below average. In statistics "speak" this is called a bell curve.

This data is significant for those who are leaders or in government. It is logical and probably necessary for the leaders in society and government come from those in the above average groups.

Obviously, society wants the most qualified to lead and govern.
While intelligence may not be the only factor, or even the most important factor in choosing leaders or those who govern, it certainly ranks high in the selection process. Yet think of the complexities of leading or governing from an extreme category when those being lead or governed are in the opposite extreme category. Conflict and distrust seem unavoidable. Unscrupulous characters and demagogues can take advantage of those in the lower category, exacerbating this inherent lack of trust in the leadership or governing group, causing them intentional long term harm for personal gain. Dictators do it all the time.

There are more questions than answers.

We do not have to have answers to these immutable questions. Perhaps we cannot answer the questions. What is important is to understand the inequality of natural selection, and to live our lives recognizing that disparity of ability and capability are part of the system of life, and of living, that is just part of the human experiment. It requires a certain sense of understanding, of acceptance, of wariness, of common sense as we go about our daily toils.

From a business perspective this statistical information can affect not only whom we hire, but, importantly, how we communicate with our work force. Not every employee has the same capacity to learn, respond to instructions or understand or carry out company policy.

As marketers our means of reaching out to customers needs to be broad enough and sufficiently varied to attract the greatest number of customers recognizing the diversity of capacity within the population.

It's not easy, but recognizing the conundrum allows the astute businessperson the opportunity for a thoughtful and comprehensive approach.